Michael Cunningham

A guide to sex discrimination and fair employment legislation in Northern Ireland

by Karen Jackson

AF841721

First published September 1977 by
The Industrial Society
PO Box 1BQ, Robert Hyde House
48 Bryanston Square, London W1H 1BQ
© 1977 The Industrial Society

ISBN 0 85290 154 2

£3.00

Contemprint Limited, London WC2

Contents

Foreword

Equality of opportunity in our society has long been an ideal for many.

Following upon the heels of legislation in the US the United Kingdom has now become subject to legislation which concerns discrimination in the employment field on grounds of sex.

The Government has seen fit to introduce similar legislation in Northern Ireland together with an additional Act concerned with fair employment.

Many organisations in Northern Ireland have followed with interest the legislation that has been introduced over a period in Great Britain and have told us how useful they find the Society's guides to the various Acts.

Karen Jackson, of the Society's Information and Personnel Advisory Service, has carried out particular assignments for organisations in Northern Ireland.

This guide attempts to put the Sex Discrimination (NI) Order and the Fair Employment (NI) Act into understandable language for employers and trade unionists, and, as usual with Society guides to legislation, not only points out the action necessary to comply with legislation but also the implications for industrial relations which arise from the activities of our representatives at Westminster.

This guide is complementary to that produced by Francis Reynolds on the Industrial Relations (NI) Orders. The Society hopes that it will be of help to all those concerned with the management of people in the Province.

PAT LENNON
Division Director

PART I

Introduction to the Sex Discrimination (Northern Ireland) Order 1976

Part	*Article*	**The Sex Discrimination (Northern Ireland) Order 1976**
II	*3 (1), 5 (1)*	This Order has two main purposes: **1** to make discrimination against any person for reasons of sex or marital status unlawful in employment, training and related matters. This would not only apply to intentional discrimination but also to practices which regardless of motive are discriminatory in effect.
II	*4 (1), 6 (3)*	The Order applies to discrimination against both women and men and references to the rights of women to equal treatment with men are to be understood as including also the rights of a man to equal treatment with women except in special circumstances.
VII	*54 (1)*	**2** to establish an Equal Opportunities Commission for Northern Ireland to: **(a)** enforce the legislation; **(b)** promote equality between the sexes generally.

Comment

The Sex Discrimination (Northern Ireland) Order 1976 is very similar to the Sex Discrimination Act which came into effect in Great Britain (excluding Northern Ireland) on 29 December 1975. The Order was effective from 1 December 1976 although certain provisions concerning the setting up of the Equal Opportunities Commission became effective from 1 September 1976.

1 *It is to be hoped, however, that the Order has more success than the Act in its first year of existence. The first twelve months of the Act's life has seen a success rate in industrial tribunals considerably lower than that for unfair dismissal cases (33 per cent) and has been the subject of considerable comment that the industrial tribunals have adhered more to the letter than the spirit of the legislation. The most striking overall conclusion from an analysis of the cases so far is that many industrial tribunals have not got to grips with the meaning and intention of sex discrimination legislation. However, it must in all fairness be said that what the law intends or means is not always what the law* says. *If the law is poorly drafted courts and tribunals can only interpret it as it stands, eg interpretation of work of* equal *value is a very precise statement and does not mean work of* greater *value.*

2 *The Commission has a general responsibility for the Order and for advising the Department of Manpower Services on the working of the Equal Pay (Northern Ireland) Act 1970. It is a principal source of information and advice for the general public and may in certain cases assist individuals who consider that they may have been discriminated against. The Commission address is:*

Equal Opportunities Commission for Northern Ireland
Lindsay House, Callender Street, Belfast BT1 5DT
(Belfast 42752)

The address of the DMS is:

Department of Manpower Services
Netherleigh, Massey Avenue, Belfast BT4 2JP
(Belfast 63244).

Part *Article*

General discrimination

II

Definitions

1 Discrimination occurs against a woman when:

3 (1a) **(a)** she is treated less favourably than a man on the grounds of her sex;

3 (1b) **(b)** she has to comply with a requirement which although it applies equally to a man, is more difficult for her to comply with and is not a genuinely necessary requirement.

4 (1) (2) The provisions should also be read as applying equally to the treatment of men except with regard to special treatment in connection with pregnancy and childbirth.

2 Discrimination occurs against a married person when:

5 (1a) **(a)** he or she is treated less favourably than an unmarried person on the grounds of his or her marital status;

5 (1b) **(b)** when he or she has to comply with a requirement which although it applies equally to married and single people is more difficult for married people to comply with and is not a genuinely necessary requirement.

6 (1) **3** Discrimination occurs when a person is victimised (or treated less favourably) for having either:

(a) brought proceedings; or

(b) given evidence or information in relation to the Sex Discrimination or Equal Pay Acts;

6 (2) unless this allegation was false.

Comment

Locator Code: KWCC01-00054
KAS0004113
Title: Guide to Sex Discrimination and Fair Employment in Northern Ireland
Condition: Used - Very Good
ISBN 9780852901540
Special Comments: ... wear
Shipment Tracking Id ...
Entered By: ...
KAS0004113

1 *In this respect* (**a**
discrimination and (
discrimination and is
persons on the grou
discrimination it is i
intended, or was aw
disproportionate adv
in a direct discrimina
An example of (**a**)
mortgages to men bu
An example of (**b**)
for employment as a
heavy weights which
of the job. Companies
recruitment and select

There are four criteria for the testing of indirect discrimination.

These are:

(**a**) *the application of a requirement or condition to men and women alike;*

(**b**) *the requirement or condition is such that the proportion of women who can comply with it is considerably smaller than the proportion of men who can;*

(**c**) *where the respondent cannot show that a requirement is justifiable irrespective of sex;*

(**d**) *where the applicant has suffered a detriment because she cannot comply.*

The result will depend on the particular circumstances of each individual case. In each case the question will be determined by the tribunal hearing the case by reference to all the facts.

The special maternity provisions of the Industrial Relations (Northern Ireland) Order No 2 are not, therefore, discriminatory.

2 *This part only applies to the employment field.*

An example of (**a**) *would be to dismiss air hostesses from their jobs upon marriage on the grounds that their work entails too much time away from home.*

An example of (**b**) *would be where a requirement of a job was that the individual had no children, eg a housekeeper.*

Part *Article*

Discrimination in the employment field

III *8 (1)*

1 By employers

It is unlawful to discriminate on the grounds of sex or marital status in relation to:

A RECRUITMENT

(a) the arrangements that are made for the purposes of determining who should be offered that employment;

8 (4) **(b)** the terms on which employment is offered (except provisions in relation to death and retirement);

(c) refusing or deliberately omitting to offer employment.

8 (2) B PRESENT EMPLOYEES

(a) what arrangements are made for training and promotion;

(b) the terms and conditions under which employment is held;

(c) dismissal, redundancy and short time.

2 By persons with statutory power to select employees for others

9 It will be unlawful for a person who is empowered by virtue of a statutory provision to select, or nominate, another person for employment by a third person to discriminate:

(a) by refusing or deliberately omitting to select or nominate a person on the grounds of sex or marital status or;

(b) where candidates are selected or nominated in order of preference by selecting or nominating a person lower in order than any other who is selected or nominated, on the grounds of sex or marital status.

Comment

1 *In this respect* **(a)** *is considered to be* direct *discrimination and* **(b)** *is considered to be* indirect *discrimination and is also applied to discrimination against persons on the grounds of marital status. In indirect discrimination it is irrelevant whether the employer intended, or was aware of, a neutral rule's disproportionate adverse effect on women (though crucial in a direct discrimination claim).*

An example of **(a)** *would be the granting of cheaper mortgages to men but not extending the facility to women.*

An example of **(b)** *would be when a women applying for employment as a packer is asked to lift exceptionally heavy weights which are not in fact a requirement of the job. Companies should carefully examine their recruitment and selection procedures, etc, in this context.*

There are four criteria for the testing of indirect discrimination.

These are:

(a) *the application of a requirement or condition to men and women alike;*

(b) *the requirement or condition is such that the proportion of women who can comply with it is considerably smaller than the proportion of men who can;*

(c) *where the respondent cannot show that a requirement is justifiable irrespective of sex;*

(d) *where the applicant has suffered a detriment because she cannot comply.*

The result will depend on the particular circumstances of each individual case. In each case the question will be determined by the tribunal hearing the case by reference to all the facts.

The special maternity provisions of the Industrial Relations (Northern Ireland) Order No 2 are not, therefore, discriminatory.

2 *This part only applies to the employment field.*

An example of **(a)** *would be to dismiss air hostesses from their jobs upon marriage on the grounds that their work entails too much time away from home.*

An example of **(b)** *would be where a requirement of a job was that the individual had no children, eg a housekeeper.*

Part *Article*

Discrimination in the employment field

III *8 (1)*

1 By employers

It is unlawful to discriminate on the grounds of sex or marital status in relation to:

A RECRUITMENT

(a) the arrangements that are made for the purposes of determining who should be offered that employment;

8 (4) **(b)** the terms on which employment is offered (except provisions in relation to death and retirement);

(c) refusing or deliberately omitting to offer employment.

8 (2) B PRESENT EMPLOYEES

(a) what arrangements are made for training and promotion;

(b) the terms and conditions under which employment is held;

(c) dismissal, redundancy and short time.

2 By persons with statutory power to select employees for others

9 It will be unlawful for a person who is empowered by virtue of a statutory provision to select, or nominate, another person for employment by a third person to discriminate:

(a) by refusing or deliberately omitting to select or nominate a person on the grounds of sex or marital status or;

(b) where candidates are selected or nominated in order of preference by selecting or nominating a person lower in order than any other who is selected or nominated, on the grounds of sex or marital status.

Comment

Some examples of such discrimination would be:

(a) *telling the switchboard to discourage possible applicants of the 'wrong' sex by saying that the job had been taken. A person has the right to unbiassed treatment during selection.*

(b) *putting excessive emphasis on difficult aspects of the job, ie lack of toilet facilities at a rarely visited site.*

Equal conditions of employment for retirement and death will not be law until the terms of the Social Security Pensions (Northern Ireland) Order 1975 come into force on 6 April 1978.

(a) *making it excessively difficult for married women to achieve either by arranging weekend courses;*

(b) *granting cheaper mortgages for one sex and not the other;*

(c) *choosing married women to be made redundant on the grounds that there is another wage earner in the family. The 'breadwinner' criterion is not a valid basis for redundancy selection.*

Under the Industrial Relations (Northern Ireland) No 1 Order Article 24(1)(a) the usual 26 weeks' continuous employment before unfair dismissal rights come into force does not apply in the case of dismissal for sex discrimination.

This provision covers, for example, the selection of certain teachers by school management committees for employment by Education and Library Boards, and the selection of certain medical and dental specialists by specially appointed panels for appointment to the Health Service by Health Boards.

Part Article

Exceptions

III 10

1 Where sex is a genuine occupational qualification

10 (1) Sex discrimination by an employer in recruiting for a job or for providing opportunities for promotion, transfer or training is unlawful except where a person's sex is a genuine occupational qualification for the job. This does not apply to married persons, or victimisation.

10 (2) A person's sex is a genuine occupational qualification for a job:

(a) where the essential nature of the job demands a certain physiology or in dramatic performances or other entertainment for reasons of authenticity;
(b) where considerations of privacy or decency or physical contact make it a requirement that persons be of a specific sex;
(c) where it is necessary for the jobholder to sleep on the premises and there are no separate sleeping or sanitary facilities available. This does not apply if the employer could *reasonably* be expected to provide separate facilities;
(d) where it is more effective that welfare facilities and/or provisions in single sex establishments be provided by a person of a specific sex;
(e) where a job needs to be held by a man because of statutory provisions imposed under present legislation;
(f) where the job involves work outside the UK in a country whose laws and customs are such that the job can only be done effectively by one of the sexes;
(g) the job is one of two to be held by a married couple.

2 In private households and small firms

8 (3) Sex discrimination and discrimination against married persons is not unlawful where:

(a) the employment in question is for the purposes of a private household;
(b) the employer does not employ a total of more than five persons.

Comment

1 *The genuine occupational qualification is not an automatic exception for general categories of jobs; in every case it will be necessary for the employer to show, if the exception is to be claimed, that the criteria set out apply to the particular job in question. In many cases the genuine occupational qualification will apply to only part of a job.*

(a) *it is important to note that this provision does not relate to physical strength or stamina. An example would be modelling clothes for physiology and a Playboy Bunny for authenticity but* not *where they were employed as croupiers;*

(b) *such jobs as tailoring and toilet attendants might come into this category although it is not a consideration on the continent where the toilet attendant for men is often a woman;*

(c) *this provision might apply to a ship where there is limited space but not to a farm where, for example, the provision of a chemical toilet would not be prohibitive;*

(d) *this might apply to hospitals, prisons and community homes for young persons and sometimes to welfare workers;*

(e) *factory legislation for example prohibits women being employed outside certain hours and on specific jobs. Certain aspects of these regulations may change, however, in the near future;*

(f) *this could apply particularly where a person's job took him/her to an Eastern country but the provisions of the Order generally do not apply if an employee does the job mainly or wholly outside Northern Ireland.*

2 *This provision does not apply to victimisation which remains unlawful in these circumstances.*

This provision refers to the total number of persons employed together with any associated employer and includes part-time persons but not those in private households.

Part	Article	3 **For reasons of childbirth, death and retirement**
		Discrimination is not unlawful where:
III	4 (2)	**(a)** there are special provisions relating to women in connection with pregnancy or childbirth; or
	8 (4)	**(b)** different provisions are made in relation to death or retirement.

4 In the place of employment

The Order does not apply where a person works wholly or mainly outside Northern Ireland.

		5 **In special employment cases**
IX	82 (5) 85 (6)	**(a)** the Order does not apply to service in the naval, military or air forces of the Crown or in which the employee may be required to serve in support of the armed services;
III	19	**(b)** service with the police is covered except in relation to height requirements and the provision of uniform and equipment;
	20	**(c)** service with the prison authorities is covered except for the different height requirements for men and women and the genuine occupational qualifications;
	22	**(d)** midwives are excepted from the Order in relation to selection, promotion, transfer and training;
	21 (1) (2)	**(e)** the Order does not apply to ministers of religion where the employment is restricted to one sex so as to comply with the doctrines of the religion or avoid offending those whose religion it is;
	23	**(f)** it remains unlawful under the Mines Act (Northern Ireland) 1969 for a woman to be employed in a job where a significant proportion of time is spent below ground.

Comment

3 *This relates to provisions of pension schemes and retirement ages.*

Similarly the Equal Pay (Northern Ireland) Act 1970 does not extend to these matters except that from 6 April 1978 it will extend to equal access to occupational pension schemes so far as such access is required by the provisions of the Social Security Pensions (Northern Ireland) Order 1975. These provisions are equal treatment for men and women in relation to conditions as to age and length of service for admission to a pension scheme and in relation to whether membership of the scheme is voluntary or obligatory.

4 *There have been some odd tribunal cases referring to these types of clauses and it is not safe to assume that this section applies in any instance.*

5 *All other provisions apply to acts done by or on behalf of the Crown.*

Employment in support of the armed services is subject to the Equal Pay (Northern Ireland) Act 1970.

It is now legal for men to become midwives. The Nurses and Midwives (Northern Ireland) Act 1970 was amended from 1 September 1976 to allow this.

It is now lawful for a woman to be employed underground in a disused mine or in employment which involves occasional duties underground in an active mine. The Coal Mines Regulations Act 1908 is amended to allow for this.

Part *Article*

Other provisions

III *14*

1 Partnerships

It would be unlawful for a firm with six or more partners to discriminate against a woman in the selection or remuneration of additional partners or to treat a woman who was already a partner any less favourably or remove her from her position on the grounds of her sex.

2 Trade unions, employer's associations and trade associations

15 The Order prohibits trade unions, employers' or trade associations from discriminating against a woman by refusing her membership or refusing to receive an application for membership, or to restrict in any way the benefits offered to women members.

16

3 Qualifying bodies

The Order prohibits an organisation which offers qualifications of any kind from placing any special restrictions on the terms under which women apply for or obtain qualifications.

18 (1)

4 Employment agencies

An employment agency would be prohibited from refusing its services to a person or offering women different terms or services. Where it is not unlawful for an employer to discriminate (genuine occupational qualification) it is correspondingly not unlawful for an agency to discriminate. The agency can act on the employers assurance of

18 (3-5) genuine occupational qualification.

5 Vocational training bodies

17 (1) (2) Training organisations, including industrial training boards, group training associations and those acting on behalf of the Department of Manpower Services, are prevented from restricting the training they offer to a woman or making it harder for women to receive training.

6 Contract workers

12 (1) (2) (3) It is unlawful for a person who contracts with another person for the services of workers employed by that other person to discriminate against a woman contract worker in the terms on which he allows her to do the work in question, continuing to do the work or the way he affords her benefits, facilities or services.

Comment

This naturally excludes partnerships where being a man is a genuine occupational qualification.

This does not apply to provision made in relation to the death or retirement from work of a member.

Such organisations will be allowed a year in which to abolish any discrimination in financial contributions or benefits connected with membership. It also provides that re-organisation of membership on a non-discriminatory basis must take place within the same period of a year, ie by January 1978. This applies particularly to membership of certain single-sex organisations in the teaching profession.

The particular provisions applicable to the enforcement of this provision are on page 20.

The agency is dependent on the employer for an assurance that it is acting in good faith in the case of a genuine occupational qualification. Where in the case of an offence the agency can show it acted in good faith its action would not be unlawful. The employer who made such an assurance could be punishable by a fine not exceeding £400.

This does not include training as a midwife.

There is an exception to permit certain kinds of 'positive action' by vocational training bodies (see page 18).

This does not occur where this is a genuine occupational qualification for a man to do the contract work.

Part | Article

Relationship between the Sex Discrimination (Northern Ireland) Order and the Equal Pay (Northern Ireland) Act 1970

III *11 (1)* Certain parts of the Equal Pay Act are amended. If the terms of a contract under which a woman is employed do not include an equality clause, they will be deemed to include one.

11 (1(2)) An equality clause is a provision which relates to terms (whether concerned with pay or not) of a contract under which a woman is employed, and has the effect that where:

(**a**) a woman is employed on like work with a man in the same employment; or

(**b**) where the woman is employed on work rated as equivalent with a man in the same employment, her contract shall be treated as modified to be no less favourable than that of the man and to include all terms that benefit the man.

11 (1(3)) The equality clause will not operate in relation to genuine material differences between one case and the other if they relate to qualifications, experience, length of service or other personal attributes (other than sex).

Comment

There is no overlap between an individual's rights under the Equal Pay Act and those under the Sex Discrimination Order. All complaints of discrimination about access to jobs and matters not included in a contract of employment, and about contractual matters (other than pay) in situations not covered by the Equal Pay Act are dealt with under the Sex Discrimination Order. For enforcement purposes it will not be necessary for a complainant to be sure which of the two enactments is relevant to their case; the tribunal will decide a case under whatever enactment is relevant.

Briefly the distinctions between the two enactments are:

EQUAL PAY

(a) *if the less favourable treatment relates to pay as regulated by the contract of employment;*

(b) *if the employee is treated less favourably than the opposite sex doing the same, broadly similar or equally evaluated work and this relates to some matter which is regulated by the contract of employment.*

SEX DISCRIMINATION

(a) *where the less favourable treatment relates to a matter not included in the contract (either expressly or implied);*

(b) *where the less favourable treatment relates to a matter other than pay in a contract and the comparison is with those* not *doing the same, broadly similar or equally evaluated work;*

(c) *where the complaint relates to a matter other than pay and regulated by a contract of employment but is based on an allegation that an employee of the other sex* would *be treated more favourably in similar circumstances.*

Of course the root of the problem is what is the 'same' or 'broadly similar' work. All employers are encouraged to introduce job evaluation schemes which can prove that any differences in pay and conditions are lawful.

Part *Article*

Other unlawful acts

1 Discriminatory practices

V 38 This provision forbids the application of a requirement or condition which results in an act of discrimination which is unlawful or which would be likely to result in such an act of discrimination if the persons to whom it applied were not all of one sex.

39 (1) **2 Advertisements**

(a) This provision makes it unlawful to publish or place for publication an advertisement which indicates or might reasonably be taken to indicate an intention to do an act which is or might be unlawful discrimination;

39 (3) **(b)** it is also unlawful to publish a job advertisement which uses a job description or title with a sexual connotation unless there is an explanation to the effect that the job is open to both men and women;

39 (4) **(c)** publishers who rely on a statement by an employer that the advertisement is made in good faith are not subject to any liability should the advertisement prove unlawful;

39 (5) **(d)** it is an offence for an employer to make a misleading statement to a publisher. A fine of up to £400 is the punishment for a conviction.

40 **3 Instructions to discriminate**

The Order makes it unlawful for a person who has authority over or influence with another person to instruct that person to do an act of unlawful discrimination.

41 **4 Pressure to discriminate**

The Order makes it unlawful for a person to bring pressure to bear on another person to do an act of unlawful discrimination whether covertly or overtly.

43 **5 Aiding unlawful acts**

Any person knowingly aiding another to discriminate is committing an unlawful act.

Comment

This complements the provisions for indirect discrimination (see page 5). Legal proceedings for contravention of all the following provisions can only be brought by the Equal Opportunities Commission for Northern Ireland.

This would not be unlawful where there was a genuine occupational qualification.

This part of the Act covers both advertisements which are specifically sex biased, eg, barmaid, waiter, salesgirl, and also where a description of the job emphasises those aspects which are only likely to appeal to a person of a particular sex, or make it clear that a person of a particular sex is preferred.

An example would be 'Bar staff required—must have particular physical attractions'.

This would apply equally well to an employer over an employee or to a company with one of its subsidiaries.

The other side of the coin to this provision is that anything done by a person in the course of his employment shall be treated as being done by the employer whether or not it was done with the employer's knowledge or approval.

Part *Article*

General exceptions and positive action

VI *48 (1)* **1 Training bodies**

Where it appears to a specified training body that at any time within the preceding twelve months there were *no* members of one sex engaged in particular work or the number was comparatively small it is lawful to discriminate on behalf of that sex as regards access to, and encouragement to undergo, training.

48 (2) This provision also applies to specific parts of Northern Ireland and not only to Northern Ireland as a whole.

48 (3) It would also not be unlawful for these bodies to discriminate on behalf of those who are in special training need because of the period for which they have been discharging domestic or family responsibilities.

48 (4) The training bodies which may take advantage of these provisions are the industrial training boards, group training associations of employers and any other person who has been designated in an Order made by the Department of Manpower Services.

49 (1) **2 Employers**

Where particular work for an employer is done exclusively by one sex or by a very limited number of a minority sex during the previous twelve months, it is lawful for an employer to provide access to facilities for that minority sex and encourage them to take advantage of any opportunity he may provide.

49 (2) (3) **3 Trade unions, employers' associations, etc**

50 (1) (2) There are a number of provisions which allow certain organisations to take positive action to ensure that members of both sexes receive training and are fully represented at various levels in the organisation, again using the twelve month rule.

Comment

This would be the Senate of a University, for example. The order does not permit 'reverse discrimination'; for example it would be unlawful to discriminate in favour of women in recruitment or promotion on the grounds that they should be allowed special treatment to make up for discrimination in the past. However, the Order does allow these forms of positive action *by specified training bodies.*

It is interesting to note that the original Bill for the Sex Discrimination Act did not contain these provisions and that it was only after lobbying by The Industrial Society and others that they were written into the Act and subsequently into the Northern Ireland Order.

This would apply particularly to married women who have given up work to bring up a family and now wish to return.

This exception does not make it lawful for the employer to discriminate at the point of selection for such work in order to achieve a balance between the sexes.

This does not allow a trade union to discriminate in favour of women when actually appointing shop stewards or to reserve a certain proportion of posts for women, but it does allow certain seats on elected bodies *to be the special preserve of an under-represented sex.*

Part *Article*

Enforcement

1 Enforcement in the employment field

VIII *63 (1)* **(a)** INDUSTRIAL TRIBUNALS

Individuals who consider that they may be the victims of discrimination have the right to institute proceedings in an industrial tribunal within three months of the date of the act complained of.

63 (2) The only exceptions to this are complaints relating to the granting of authorisations or qualifications where there is already a statutory procedure for appeal.

(b) CONCILIATION

64 (1) Where the parties request it or where it believes it could be of assistance, the Labour Relations Agency can provide the services of a conciliation officer whose duty it would be to promote a settlement. Information
64 (4) given to a conciliation officer by either party may not be divulged at a tribunal without their consent.

(c) ASSISTANCE BY EQUAL OPPORTUNITIES COMMISSION

75 The Order gives the Equal Opportunities Commission for Northern Ireland the opportunity to assist an individual making a complaint but only where the case:

(i) raises a question of principle
(ii) is too complex for the individual to handle, or
(iii) some other consideration arises.

74 **(d)** HELP FOR AGGRIEVED PERSONS

The Order allows persons who feel they may have been discriminated against to use a standard form on which they can question the person they are complaining against.

65 (1) **(e)** REMEDIES

(2) (3) Where a tribunal decides in favour of the complainant it may:

(i) make an order declaring the rights of the complainant
(ii) make an order for compensation

Comment

Industrial tribunals sit in different parts of the Province as required. Each tribunal has a legally qualified chairman and two lay members who are experienced in labour relations. The burden of proof is on the complainant to show that he or she has been treated less favourably by virtue of sex or marital status. It is then for the respondent to seek to rebut this evidence.

This would be the Senate of a University, for example.

In ordinary cases an individual may seek professional help and advice from a union or a member of the legal professions. Legal aid, however, does not apply to tribunals.

It is in the interest of an employer who is sent one of these forms (SD74) to answer it and quickly, or his failure to do so may have a harmful effect at a subsequent industrial tribunal case, where it may be produced as evidence.

It is important to distinguish between the different types of offence under the Sex Discrimination Order and the different types of compensation that may be payable.

Double compensation for unfair dismissal and discrimination is not possible and thus in unfair dismissal cases the compensation would be a maximum of £2,400 basic, a maximum of £5,200 compensatory and a maximum of £4,160 punitive where the employer fails to carry out a recommendation for re-instatement and re-engagement.

In a case of discrimination only, a maximum of £5,200 would be payable.

Part *Article*

(iii) make a recommendation that remedial action be taken by the employer.

(f) APPEALS

There is a right of appeal *on a point of law* against a decision of an industrial tribunal.

2 Enforcement arrangements in relation to discriminatory practices and pressure and instructions to discriminate

72 (1) (2) The formal investigation and non-discrimination notice procedure are available to the Commission to deal with discriminatory advertisements and pressure and instructions to discriminate. The Commission also has special powers to institute legal proceedings for such contraventions of the Order. These may be:

(a) an application for a decision whether the alleged contravention occurred; or

(b) in order to prevent a further contravention, an application to a county court for an injunction.

Comment

Appeals are at present considered by the Court of Appeal.

For detailed information concerning the powers of the Commission see page 24.

Part *Article*

Equal Opportunities Commission for Northern Ireland

VII

Duties

54 (1) **1** 'to work towards the elimination of discrimination

2 to promote equality of opportunity between men and women generally

3 to keep under review this Order and the Equal Pay Act and when required or considered necessary to draw up proposals amending them

55 (1) **4** to undertake or assist any research and any educational activities which appear necessary or expedient

56 (1) (2) (3) **5** to keep under review any relevant statutory provisions which affect men and women and report accordingly on possible amendments

57 (1) **6** to conduct formal investigations conducive to the carrying out of its other duties.

Establishment

54 (1) (2) The Commission will have between six and twelve Commissioners including a chairman and one or two deputy chairmen. All Commissioners are appointed by the head of the Department of Manpower Services.

Powers

57 (1) **1** FORMAL INVESTIGATIONS

(a) The Commission may conduct formal investigations on its own initiative and also when requested by the Department of Manpower Services for any purposes conducive to the carrying out of its duties.

58 (3) The Commission must have terms of reference for these investigations although these may be revised. Except the investigation is confined to named persons, a 'general notice' of the holding of the investigation must be given, eg by newspaper advertisements.

59 (1) (2) **(b)** The Order empowers the Commission in certain circumstances to serve a notice requiring a person to produce relevant information either orally or in

59 (3) writing. The rules of evidence are similar to those required in civil proceedings in the High Court

Comment

In its early stages the greatest need for the Commission will be in the supplying of literature, information and will fulfil a public relations role. Later, as public understanding grows, it will be able to turn its attention to positive education, recommendations and research.

The Equal Opportunities Commission in Great Britain has not yet completed one piece of employment investigation although it has taken evidence on the statutory legislation as regards women under the Factories Acts both in respect of hours of work and specific job-related tasks at present restricted to men. Its recommendations on some aspects of these are expected in 1977.

It is to be hoped that the Equal Opportunities Commission for Northern Ireland will give guidance to industrial tribunals which has been lacking in Great Britain, based on cases already heard in Great Britain.

The Chairman of the Commission is Mrs. Margot Neill. The Deputy Chairman is Mrs Claire Kennedy (a solicitor and chairman of the Northern Ireland Electricity Consumers Council). General Manager is Mr William Marshall (Barrister-at-law).

There are at present nine Commissioners.

No investigations have as yet been completed in Great Britain.

Part	Article	
		and a person cannot be expected to attend without being given the appropriate expenses.
	59 (5)	The punishment for destroying written evidence or knowingly making false statements is a maximum fine of £400.

2 NON-DISCRIMINATION NOTICES

67 (2)	**(a)**	the Commission can serve non-discrimination notices;
67 (5)	**(b)**	the Commission must let the recipient know that it intends to serve a non-discrimination notice and give them an opportunity to make representation against it;
67 (2)	**(c)**	the notice once served requires the recipient to make changes to his practices and let the persons concerned know;
68 (1)	**(d)**	the recipient can appeal in cases of employment provisions and equal pay to an industrial tribunal or County Court;
70 (1) (2)	**(e)**	a register of non-discrimination notices must be kept which may be inspected by any person;
71	**(f)**	when final, a non-discrimination notice renders the recipient liable, if he persists for the next five years, for an injunction or court order requiring compliance.

3 SPECIAL ENFORCEMENT ARRANGEMENTS

38 (3) *72 (1) (2)*	**(a)**	The Commission has special powers and functions in relation to the provisions dealing with discriminatory practices and advertisements and pressure and instructions to discriminate. Legal proceedings in respect of contraventions of these provisions may be instituted *only* by the Commission.

Comment

None of these non-discrimination notices have been served in Great Britain.

The recipient has a period of not less than 28 days to do this in.

The recipient must do this within six weeks of receiving the notice.

Aggrieved individuals have the right of direct access to the industrial tribunals in respect of employment practice and equal pay.

The Commission may in special circumstances give assistance (see page 20).

Action by management

The Order has major implications for all industries but particularly those with a traditionally exclusive workforce of one sex or another. Employers will not be able to aim their recruitment at any particular sex or be able to bar women from promotion or careers training. It will provide constraints within which management must work but although it also provides penalties it will only be effective if managements can develop positive attitudes and rid themselves of deeply rooted traditions, prejudices and customs which have existed for generations.

Managements have a threefold responsibility—to the company, to the employee and to the legislation—and in order to fulfil all of these must develop a positive action programme to ensure the optimum utilisation of all the skills and knowledge of individuals within the company.

Plan of action

1 Establish the current position, practices and procedures by examining:

(a) the proportion of male and female employees at each level of responsibility and in each pay group;

(b) the application of employee benefits and terms and conditions of employment between men and women;

(c) reasons for the differences—historical, physical, educational or skill;

(d) recruitment and selection procedures;

(e) promotion and training activities.

2 Take positive action:

- ensure that there is maximum publicity concerning the new legislation
- communicate what the new rights are, particularly to women
- check that advertisements make no reference to sex or marital status unless it is a genuine occupational qualification
- check application forms are the same for men and women
- select or prepare women for training in traditionally male departments
- analyse jobs to ensure that the correct factors are being emphasised

- ensure appointments are being made on the basis of ability and qualification
- make training available equally to men and women except where imbalance makes it necessary to train one particular sex
- check that there is evaluation between salaries and wages and that there are not discriminating factors
- check employee benefits—loans, mortgages, medical and sick pay schemes and relocation allowances
- check redundancy or security of employment schemes
- make sure that records are kept for six months with reasons for recruitment and promotion rejects.

3 No piece of legislation works in isolation and the Sex Discrimination (Northern Ireland) Order, 1976 overlaps with other employment legislation, including:
The Industrial Relations (Northern Ireland) Orders 1976
The Equal Pay (Northern Ireland) Act 1970
The Social Security Pensions (Northern Ireland) Order 1975
The Contracts of Employment and Redundancy Payments (Northern Ireland) Act 1965.

PART II

Introduction to The Fair Employment (Northern Ireland) Act 1976

Part *Section*

I

This Act has three main purposes:

1 to promote equality of opportunity in employment in Northern Ireland between persons of different religious beliefs

2 to make religious and political discrimination in employmcnts and occupations unlawful

3 to establish a Fair Employment Agency with the function of promoting equality of opportunity and securing remedies for unlawful discrimination.

It entitles persons who consider they have suffered from such discrimination in employment to submit claims to the Agency.

It enables the Agency to conduct investigations into employment practices which may be discriminatory.

Comment

The Fair Employment (Northern Ireland) Act 1976 is unique and nothing like it exists in the rest of the United Kingdom.

Unlike the Sex Discrimination (Northern Ireland) Order 1976 the Act only applies to religious and political discrimination within the employment field.

The Act was effective from 1 December 1976 although certain provisions concerning the establishment of the Fair Employment Agency became effective 1 September 1976.

To keep the workload of the Fair Employment Agency within reasonable limits, employers of fewer than 26 persons will be outside the scope of the Act until 31 August 1978, and employers of fewer than 11 persons until 31 August 1979.

Part *Section*

The Fair Employment Agency for Northern Ireland

I *1 (1)* **A Duties**

1 to promote equality of opportunity in Northern Ireland

2 to work for the elimination of religious and political discrimination in employments and occupations

2 (1) **3** to undertake any research and fulfil various educational functions particularly by holding training courses and conferences and providing information about its activities

24 (1) **4** to conduct formal investigations into individual complaints

11 **5** to identify and keep under review patterns and trends in employment

12 (1) (2) **6** to investigate and remedy practices which fail to afford equality of opportunity

B Establishment .

1 and schedule 1 The Agency must have a chairman and not less than five and no more than eleven members appointed by the Head of the Department of Manpower Services.

C Powers

11 **1 Patterns of employment**

It is the duty of the Agency to identify and keep under review patterns of employment in Northern Ireland for the purposes of:

(a) considering whether equality of opportunity exists and where it does not;

(b) considering how equality of opportunity can best be achieved;

(c) where such equality is absent, the reasons for its absence.

Comment

In its early stages the Agency will be concerned to publicise itself and its work. It will also be concerned to encourage employers to sign the Declaration of Intent and so compile the Register of Fair Employers.

Later it will produce findings on individual allegations and more literature designed to help employers in a positive way.

The Agency is an independent body financed by the Department of Manpower Services. The Chairman of the Agency is Mr Robert G Cooper, a former Minister of Manpower in the Northern Ireland government. Mr Cooper, who is qualified in law, is also a member of the Standing Advisory Committee on Human Rights. The Agency's address is:

> *The Fair Employment Agency for Northern Ireland*
> *Lindsay House, Callender Street*
> *Belfast BT1 5DT*
> *Telephone: Belfast 40020.*

One way of assessing this would be to investigate the ratio of persons of different religious beliefs in any employment, which would normally reflect the same ratio as in an employment catchment area. This in itself would not be conclusive, however, bearing in mind the 'material differences' clauses.

Some practices may in fact be discriminatory without the intention being so, eg using an unnecessarily restricted catchment area for recruitment where the residents are of a particular religious belief.

Part	Section	
	12 (1) (2)	**2 Formal investigations of employment practices**

(a) the Agency is empowered to conduct investigations into certain practices by those over whom the Act has jurisdiction. They are:

II 12 (1)

1 Employers
2 Persons empowered by statute to select people for employment by others
3 Employment agencies
4 Trade unions and employers' organisations
5 Persons providing services connected with training for employments or occupations
6 Persons who confer qualifications for engaging in employments or occupations.

(b) for the same purpose the Agency may investigate the composition by reference to religious beliefs of those over whom the Act has jurisdiction. They are:

1 Persons who have applied for or obtained employment by any employer
2 Persons who have applied for or obtained the services of any employment agency
3 Persons who have applied for or obtained membership of any vocational organisation
4 Persons who have sought or obtained the services of bodies providing training
5 Persons who have sought or have had conferred on them qualifications to engage in employments or occupations.

Comment

The practices include recruitment and membership policies, promotion policies and services provided by training organisations and employment agencies.

Where employers and others hold this information they will be required to produce it but the Act does not require employers and others to keep records of religious beliefs. Additionally the Act provides specifically that no one can be compelled to produce information from which his own religious beliefs can be deduced if he objects to doing so.

The Agency does not have to have received a complaint in order to initiate investigations.

Part Section

Equality of opportunity

Definitions

II *3 (1)* **1** 'Equality of opportunity' means equality of opportunity between persons of different religious beliefs.

3 (2) **2** A person of any religious belief has equality of opportunity with a person of any other religious belief if being:

(a) a person who is seeking employment or is in employment; or

(b) a person who is seeking to become engaged in or is engaged in any occupation,

he has the same opportunity as that other person due allowance being made for any material difference in their suitability.

3 (3a) **3** The kinds of opportunity are:

(a) to be considered and to be submitted for consideration for employment;

(b) to have it and hold it on any terms;

(c) to have access to all benefits connected with it and without being subjected to any detriment.

3 (3b) **4** The same rights apply to:

(a) any vocational organisation;

(b) where services in connection with training for the employment are provided by a person other than the employer;

(c) having conferred on him, to hold, any qualifications needed for engagement.

Comment

It is only just that employers and others should have their rights to assess suitability on the basis of individual merit protected, and that is what 'due allowance being made for any material differences in their suitability' means. Obviously if one individual is more suited to a job than another their religious views are both immaterial to their selection and to their ability to do the job. Companies should carefully examine their recruitment, selection and promotion policies in this context.

It is always a wise precaution in any selection procedure to make notes as to why certain candidates were not selected. In the event of any allegations being brought, these notes could be produced as evidence that there was some material difference between the candidates which led to one and not the other being chosen.

Now that selection needs to be capable of being justified it is most important to be sure that proper methods and procedures are used. If an employer is unable to demonstrate that he uses a suitable and effective system for selection he is going to have problems in showing that alleged discrimination did not take place.

Part *Section*

Unlawful discrimination

Definitions

III *16 (2)* **1** Discrimination occurs against a person when he/she is treated less favourably on the ground of religious belief or political opinion than the person concerned would treat someone else in the same circumstances.

16 (3) **2** Discrimination occurs when a person is victimised (or is treated less favourably) for having:

(a) made a complaint under the Act;

(b) given evidence in connection with a complaint or proceedings under the Act;

(c) alleged that the victimiser or someone else has contravened the Act;

(d) taken any action under or by reference to the Act;

16 (4) unless this allegation was false otherwise than in good faith

Comment

1 *Any employer is entitled to take into account the ability, personal characteristics, or other attributes of an applicant which are relevant in assessing suitability for the job, promotion or training in question.*

2 *Individuals who feel that they have been discriminated against or who feel that discrimination has taken place are protected from further or subsequent discrimination. The less favourable treatment of people who have made false allegations of discrimination does not contravene the Act.*

The protection of people who have made allegations of discrimination is not removed unless the allegation was both false and *made in bad faith.*

Part *Section*

Discrimination in the employment field

A By employers

17 (a) It is unlawful for an employer to discriminate:

(a) where a person is seeking employment:
- (i) in the arrangements the employer makes for the purpose of determining who should be offered employment
- (ii) by refusing or deliberately omitting to offer the person employment for which he applies
- (iii) in the terms on which he offers him employment;

17 (b) **(b)** where the person is employed:
- (i) in the terms of employment which he affords him
- (ii) in the way he affords him access to benefits or by refusing or deliberately omitting to afford him access
- (iii) dismissal, redundancy and short time
- (iv) subjecting him to any other detriment.

B Discrimination against contract workers

II *18 (1) (2)* It is unlawful for a person who contracts with another person for the services of workers employed by that person to discriminate against them in the terms on which he allows them to do the work in question, continuing to do the work or the way he affords them benefits, facilities or services.

C Discrimination by persons with statutory power to select employees for others

19 (a) (b) It is unlawful for a person who is empowered by virtue of a statutory provision to select or nominate another person for employment by a third person to discriminate:

(a) by refusing or deliberately omitting to select or nominate a person on the grounds of religious belief or political opinion;

(b) where candidates are selected or nominated in order of preference by selecting or nominating a person lower in order than any other who is selected or nominated on the grounds of religious belief or political opinion.

Comment

Examples of such discrimination:

(i) advertising in specific publications known to be favoured by persons of certain religious beliefs under certain circumstances;
(ii) ignoring or losing any application or letter requesting consideration;
(iii) making the job sound particularly unattractive for whatever reason.

(i) differences in holidays;
(ii) refusing access to particular benevolent funds;
(iii) choosing people of a particular belief for redundancy on the grounds that they will easily get another job.

If an employer felt that there was a material reason why persons for whom he has contracted should not be employed this would be for him to take up with the contractor in the usual way. Discrimination in this area would cover pressure from his own workers not to employ certain contract workers.

This provision covers, for example, the selection of teachers by school management committees for employment by Education and Library Boards and the selection of certain medical and dental specialists by specially appointed panels for appointment to the Health Service by Health Boards. There is, however, an exemption applying to the employment of teachers (see page 46).

Part *Section*

D Discrimination by employment agencies

It is unlawful for an employment agency to discriminate against a person:

20 (1) (**a**) in the terms on which it offers to provide any of its services;

(**b**) by refusing or deliberately omitting to provide any of its service;

(**c**) in the way it provides any of its services.

II *20 (3)* It is not unlawful for an agency to discriminate in relation to employment which the employer could lawfully refuse to offer the person concerned and there is no liability if it can show that it acted in reliance on a
20 (4) statement on which it was reasonable for it to rely.

E Discrimination by vocational organisations

21 (a) It is unlawful for a vocational organisation to discriminate:

(**a**) against those who are not members by

(i) refusing or deliberately omitting to accept their application for membership or

(ii) in the terms on which they are prepared to admit them;

(**b**) against members

(i) in the way they afford them access to benefits

(ii) by depriving them of membership or varying the terms on which they are members.

F Discrimination by persons providing training services

22 (1) It is unlawful for a person who provides training services to discriminate:

(**a**) where another person is seeking to obtain those services

(i) by refusing or deliberately omitting to provide those services or

(ii) in the terms on which the person offers to provide those services;

(**b**) where another person is receiving those services

(i) in the way the services are provided

(ii) in the way access to benefits is afforded

(iii) by withdrawing those services from him or varying the terms.

Comment

This provision includes guidance on careers and any other services related to employment.

An example of discrimination would be making a reference from a particular body or bodies a prerequisite to being put on the books or being offered to other employers.

There are exemptions to the law on discrimination where religious belief or political opinion is a genuine occupational qualification (see page 46).

Persons knowingly giving misleading information in this respect may be fined up to £400.

Vocational organisations cover trade unions and employers organisations besides professional bodies, societies and institutes.

Part	Section	
III	*23*	**G Discrimination by qualifying bodies** The Act prohibits an organisation which offers qualifications of any kind from placing any special restrictions: **(a)** by refusing or deliberately omitting to confer a qualification on application; **(b)** in the terms under which they are prepared to confer the qualification; **(c)** by withdrawing it or varying the terms under which it is held.
	24 (5)	Complainants cannot make use of the Act if there is an existing appeals procedure through the Courts.

Comment

Exceptions

Part	Section	
		1 Clergymen and ministers of religion
V	*37 (1) (a)*	Employment or occupation as a clergyman or minister of a religious denomination is exempt.
	37 (1) (b)	**2 Private households**
		Employment in private households is exempt.
	37 (3)	**3 Genuine occupational qualifications (GOQs)**
		The Act does not prohibit religious or political discrimination where the essential nature of the job requires it to be done by persons holding or not holding particular religious beliefs or political opinions.
	37	**4 Small employers**
	(4) (a) (b)	Employers of 25 persons are exempt until 31 August 1978. Employers of not more than ten people are exempt until 31 August 1979.
	37 (1) (c)	**5 Employment as a schoolteacher**
		The employment of school teachers is exempt but this is subject to review by the Fair Employment Agency
	38 (1) (2) (3) (4)	which is required to consider whether it should promote equality of opportunity in this area.
		6 Other exemptions
V	*40*	**(a)** charities;
	41	**(b)** acts done under statutory authority;
	42 (1)	**(c)** acts done for the purposes of national security, public safety and public order.

Comment

It would be up to the employer to show that he was not discriminating by proving that certain political opinions or religious beliefs were required in order to do the job.

This is to enable small employers to understand the legislation and put it into effect over a longer period and to prevent the Agency from being swamped. By 31 August 1979 the Act will apply irrespective of the numbers employed.

At the present moment segregated schools make religious beliefs a GOQ for some school teachers. However, the Agency has the power to investigate this area and report its finding to the Secretary of State.

Part *Section*

The Declaration of Principle and Intent

II *6 (1) (2)* The Agency is required to invite organisations to subscribe to a Declaration of Principle and Intent but the Act does not oblige them to do so.

The register of equal opportunity employers and organisations

7 (1) The Agency is required to keep a register of all persons who subscribe to the Declaration of Principle and Intent. All organisations who do so are entitled to receive a certificate.

7 (2) The Agency may require organisations to reaffirm the Declaration from time to time and it may remove from the register all those who fail to reaffirm or honour its terms.

7 (3) (4) Declarants who are removed from the register have the right of appeal. The Agency must inform the declarant of this right and require the return of the certificate.

Publication of the register

7 (5) The register is open to public inspection and any person is entitled to obtain a copy of the register or any entry in it.

9 (1) The Agency is required to publicise the names on the register and at yearly intervals notify various public authorities of the names of employers on the register.

9 (3) The Agency must also inform the authorities if any name is removed and the authorities inform the Agency if any organisation is acting in a way inconsistent with the terms of the Declaration.

Comment

The terms of the Declaration are as follows:

'I/We affirm and declare that it is my/our intent to promote and protect equality of opportunity in employment, according to the letter and spirit of the Fair Employment (Northern Ireland) Act 1976 by every means at my/our disposal, and to co-operate to that end with the Fair Employment Agency for Northern Ireland.

I/We undertake that I/We will use my/our best endeavours to encourage all persons within the range of my/our influence to commit themselves to the same intent.'

The Agency has very limited powers to accept alternatives to the wording of the Declaration. It is possible to obtain from the Agency a copy of the Declaration with the alternatives which they have found it possible to accept.

By July 1977 approximately 1,800 letters of invitation had been sent to employers of over 25 people. About 1,000 have signed it.

The certificate describes signatories as an 'Equal Opportunity Employer' or 'Equal Opportunity Organisation' and they can so describe themselves, eg on headed paper or in advertisements.

It is an offence carrying a maximum fine of £100 for an organisation to describe itself as an 'Equal Opportunity Employer' or an 'Equal Opportunity Organisation' or give the impression that it is one. Refusal to return the certificate is punishable by a fine of up to £100.

For more information about appeals boards, etc, see page 61.

The public authorities include all government departments, local authorities and most bodies operating in the public sector of employment, eg The Northern Ireland Electricity Service, the Housing Executive and the various area boards operating in the health and education boards. To date it has been issued to between 70 and 80 bodies.

The Act does not require public authorities to give preference to signatories.

Part *Section*

The guide to manpower policy and practice

II *5 (1)* After consultation with the Standing Advisory Commission on Human Rights and the Agency, and other appropriate interests, the Department of Manpower Services will publish and promote a guide to good manpower policy and practice.

5 (4)
14 (6) Adoption of the recommendations in the guide is voluntary. However, the Agency and the appeals board are required to give due weight to the contents of the guide when considering whether equality of opportunity is or is not being afforded.

Comment

The guide will contain recommendations which, if adopted by employers and vocational organisations will in the opinion of the Department promote equality of opportunity.

In this respect the guide will be used in the same way as a Code of Practice in that not adhering to the Code does not in itself constitute an offence. However, it will be used as a yardstick for assessing conduct. A draft guide is at the moment being circulated and will be issued in the late summer of 1977.

Part *Section*

Other unlawful acts

A Discriminatory advertisements

IV *33 (1)* **1** It is unlawful to publish or to cause to be published an advertisement which indicates an intention to commit an act of unlawful discrimination.

36 (1) **2** The County Court may, at the request of the Agency, make orders restraining persons from publishing such advertisements.

33 (3) **3** A publisher of an unlawful advertisement would not be found liable if it can be shown that he acted in good faith in reliance on the advertiser and that it was reasonable for him to do so.

B Accessories and incitement

34 (1) **1** A person who knowingly aids or incites, or who directs, procures or induces another to discriminate will be treated as though he had done it.

34 (3) **2** There is a defence for those who acted in good faith if it was reasonable for them to do so.

C Liability of employers and principals

II *35 (1) (3)* **1** Unless employers take reasonable steps to prevent acts of discrimination being done by their employees, they will be treated as though they themselves had done those acts.

35 (2) **2** Unlawful acts committed by agents, whether express or implied, will be treated as though they were acts of the principals as well as the agents.

Comment

Advertisement in this context means every form of advertisement including through notices, circulars, posters, radio, television and films as well as through newspapers or other publications.

An example of such an advertisement would be where there was a request for specific references to accompany an application.

People who make false statements are liable to fines of up to £400.

Such persons could be required to provide the same remedies for the unlawful acts as the person who had actually done it.

People who make false statements are liable to fines of up to £400.

'Inducement' means also 'intimidation'. The Act does not prejudice the operation of the criminal law in relation to intimidation.

In practical terms this means that employers must be on the lookout for both overt and covert acts of discrimination among their employees and that they themselves must not be affected by threats.

Part *Section*

Enforcement

A Remedying practices which do not afford equality of opportunity

II *13 (1)* **1** Where the Agency forms the opinion, after an investigation, that an individual has failed to afford equality of opportunity, it is obliged to come to some agreement for its remedy and where action is promised to seek a written undertaking to that effect.

13 (2) **2** Where the individual is unwilling or does not comply with an undertaking, the Agency can either serve a notice on him or enforce the undertaking in the County Court.

B Modification or revocation of directions

13 (5) On written application of the person concerned, certain provisions may be modified if the Agency feels that the argument put forward by the individual allows this or that the necessity for action no longer exists.

C Enforcement of undertaking and directions

15 (1) Undertakings and directions which are not complied with are enforceable on application by the Agency to the County Court.

43 (1) No other person may take action in the courts to achieve compliance.

15 (2) The Agency may not apply to the court for enforcement until the 21 days allowed for appeal have expired. It may not take action until any appeal has been heard or abandoned.

Comment

On some occasion, the discrimination will have been unintentional on the part of the individual and once the likely results of any acts are pointed out to him the individual will be only too willing to comply.

The notice must contain directions to take such action as it considers reasonable and appropriate for promoting equality of opportunity and also inform the individual of his rights of appeal (see Appeal Board, page 61).

Remedies

The remedies which may be obtained for failure to provide equality of opportunity are of a general nature such as the altering of employment practices.

It is important to note that the Act does not enable the Agency to impose a pattern of quotas. This in fact would be unlawful and contrary to the concept of equality of opportunity. Remedies for particular individuals (in the form of compensation) can be obtained only by means of a complaint of unlawful discrimination.

Failure to comply with an injunction could in the last resort be dealt with as contempt of court.

These restrictions do not apply to the enforcement of an undertaking. The time limit allowed for the enforcement of an undertaking is a matter for the Agency to decide at its discretion.

Part *Section*

Complaints of unlawful discrimination

III *24 (1) (2)* *43*

1 Individual complaints

Individuals who consider that they may be victims of discrimination can only apply for a remedy through a complaint to the Fair Employment Agency. This must be in writing.

24 (3)

2 Time limits

Complaints must normally be made within two months from the date on which the complainant knew of the alleged discrimination or within six months of the date on which the action occurred whichever is the earlier.

24 (1)

3 Investigations

The Agency is obliged to investigate any complaint to it made in writing unless it considers it frivolous and is given wide powers for the purpose of conducting its investigations.

Sch 5 These include:

(**a**) *para 2* notifying the persons whose practices it intends to examine in writing, whether it be an investigation of employment practices or investigating a complaint of religious or political discrimination;

(**b**) *para 3* letting such persons above know either the particular scope and purpose of the investigation or any evidence supporting the allegation.

(**c**) *Sch 5 para 4* giving those complained against the opportunity to comment on the allegations and/or provide the Agency with evidence;

(**d**) *para 8* having the same powers and being subject to the same limitations as the High Court as regards the attendance and examination of witnesses, the administration of oaths or affirmations and the production of documents;

(**e**) *para 11* paying expenses;

(**f**) *para 12* being forbidden to disclose information except such as is necessary to enable the Agency to perform its function under the Act.

Comment

Where the complainant has died or is unable to act for himself the complaint may be continued by a person acting on his behalf.

To date twenty individual allegations have been made.

The Agency has discretion to investigate complaints not made within the time limits where it considers there are special circumstances.

The Act is very careful to ensure that any information concerning an individual's religious beliefs is kept as confidential as possible.

Part Section

Findings, conciliation and enforcement of remedies

III 25 (1)

A Findings

On completing an investigation of a complaint the Agency is required to give a finding as to whether or not there has been unlawful discrimination.

25 (1)

B Conciliation

Whether or not it has found unlawful discrimination the Agency must attempt to conciliate between the parties. Where the Agency conciliatcs in a case of unlawful discrimination it must secure a written undertaking from the respondent to comply with the settlement.

25 (2)

C Reports

The Agency must inform the parties of its findings as soon as possible and also let the complainant know of any settlement and its terms.

30 (1)

D Remedies and damages

30 (1) **1** Where unlawful discrimination has been committed but not remedied the Agency may take the case to the county court on behalf of the complainant.

III 30 (4) **2** The court is entitled to:

(a) award damages; or

(b) grant an injunction; or

(c) both; and

(d) give its reasons.

31 (1) **3** Damages are awarded to compensate the complainant for any loss or injury which he has suffered. Compensation will be reduced if a complainant fails to take action to reduce his loss.

31 (2) **4** Compensation may be increased where a respondent fails to comply with a settlement etc.

32 (1) **5** The court may revise contracts which contravene the Act.

48 **6** There is a right of appeal to the Court of Appeal against decrees of the county court.

Comment

It is only after a few of these findings have been published that organisations will have some knowledge as to the types of complaint being made and the remedies being secured by the Agency.

To date no findings have been published.

As in cases of investigation the Agency can revoke or modify recommendations as it thinks fit.

It must also inform the parties of their right to appeal to the county court within 21 days of hearing the finding. The county court may quash the complaint or refer the case back to the Agency or dismiss the appeal if it agrees with the Agency's findings.

The Agency must always allow time for undertakings or recommendations to be complied with and for appeals to take place.

Damages would be at the discretion of the judge. There is no laid-down amounts, for example, in unfair dismissal cases at industrial tribunals.

A complainant would be, for example, expected to look for another job if refusal to give him a job had been the original cause of the complaint.

Part *Section*

Other provisions

Public sector and Crown employment

VI *50, 53* **1** The Act applies to the public as well as the private sector of employment including government departments, the police and armed forces.

54 **2** Where the Agency finds that employment practices in the public sector do not afford equality of opportunity and it cannot get a remedy, it must send a report on the matter to the Minister of the Head of the Department concerned who must lay it before Parliament.

Part *Section*

The Fair Employment Appeals Board

4 (1) **1 Composition**

The Fair Employment Appeals Board consists of a chairman and two other members appointed by the Head of the Department of Manpower Services. One of the members must be a barrister or solicitor of not less than seven years standing.

2 Function

To hear appeals against:

(a) removal of names from or refusal to restore names to the register of persons who have signed the Declaration of Principle and Intent;

(b) directions served by the Agency requiring action for the promotion of equality of opportunity.

Sch 4 (5) **3 Special provisions**

(a) appeals must be conducted in private;

Sch 2 (4) **(b)** in general the Board is entitled to regulate its own procedure although it is required to afford every person who appeals to it to be able to put forward relevant evidence an opportunity of being heard;

Sch 4 (3) (4) **(c)** both the appellant and Agency are entitled to appear before the Board, to be represented by counsel or solicitor and to examine their witnesses and cross-examine each other's;

Sch 4 (7) **(d)** the Board has the same powers as the High Court to require the production of relevant information or documents;

Sch 4 (8) **(e)** obstruction of the Board or contempt may be referred to the High Court which may deal with the offence as if it had been made against the High Court;

Sch 4 (10) **(f)** the Board must notify both the appellant and the Agency of its decisions and must give reasons;

Sch 4 (9) **(g)** the Board may pay expenses to those attending other than the Agency and those acting on its behalf.

Action by management

The Act has major implications on employment throughout Northern Ireland in that its avowed intent is to prevent unlawful discrimination on the grounds of religious belief or political opinions and to ensure equality of opportunity for individuals irrespective of their religious beliefs. It provides constraints within which managements must work and although it also provides penalties it will only be effective if managements can develop positive attitudes and can rid themselves of deeply rooted traditions, prejudices and customs which have existed for generations.

Managements have a three-fold responsibility—to the company, existing and prospective employees and to the law— and in order to fulfil all of these must develop a positive action programme to ensure the optimum utilisation of all the skills and knowledge within the company and the possible recruitment of it from outside.

Plan of action

1 Sign the Declaration of Principle and Intent and communicate to all employees that this has been done.

2 Let all prospective employees know you are an 'Equal Opportunity Employer' by having it printed on letter-headings and in advertisements.

3 Place the certificate describing you as an 'Equal Opportunity Employer' in a prominent place where it can be seen by as many people as possible, eg the canteen.

4 Examine the current position, practices and procedures on all recruitment, selection and promotion procedures.

5 Check that all advertisements are placed in newspapers and journals covering as wide a spread of the population as possible.

6 Ensure appointments are being made on the basis of ability and qualification.

7 Make sure that records, of recruitment and promotion rejects, are kept for six months with reasons for rejection.

8 Ensure that no manager or supervisor is keeping quotas of religious groups.

9 Discuss a strategy with senior management in the event of industrial unrest following pressure being brought to bear in some quarter.

10 Where necessary begin a programme of education and discussion on the legislation, particularly among supervisors and trade unionists.
11 Write an equal opportunity policy which covers all types of discrimination including sex and race.
12 Obtain a copy of the *Guide to manpower policy and practice* which will be published by the Department of Manpower Services and check it with your own practices.